This book is dedicated to Bill Nance
whose selfless dedication to the project made this book possible.

Through the
GARDEN GATE

The Gardens of Historic Huntsville

Donna McPherson Castellano

Photography by Charles Seifried • Design by Betty Altherr Howard

Credits

Author	Donna McPherson Castellano
Photographer	Charles Seifried
Designer	Betty Altherr Howard
Copy Editor	Jeannie Robison
Assistants	Katie Castellano
	Nathan Castellano

*Photographs by Betty Altherr Howard
on pages 10 right, 36 left, 39, 40, 47,
61 top left, 89, 107, 114, 117.*

*Printed in China through
Integrated Communications
Gardena, California*

ISBN 0-9767083-0-2 (cloth)

Contents

Foreword

The city of Huntsville can lay claim to one of the South's premier historic residential areas. Fanning eastward from the old downtown commercial district toward the lower slopes of Monte Sano Mountain, it is an area graced by dozens of landmark buildings, ranging from modest cottages to pillared mansions and venerable old churches. Blanketed in summer's green or autumn's crimson and gold, it is also an area that seems at once timeless and ever-changing.

Here, where the last spurs of the Appalachians dissolve into the great basin of the Tennessee River Valley, nature has been bountiful. The climate is temperate, the land fertile and well-watered. And so we find in the midst of an expanding city a perfect natural garden spot, ready-made for man's own horticultural handiwork and conducive to a mellow blending of landscape with architecture—a place that through nearly two centuries has slowly evolved a character all its own.

From a tight, courthouse-centered grid laid out in 1809 just above the "Big Spring," narrow streets glide away seamlessly into quiet, tree-shaded neighborhoods. Some of the streets bear revered names of the young American republic— Adams, Franklin, Randolph. Others honor early territorial officials and local grandees—Holmes, Echols, McClung. And walking the streets is like a stroll through a couple of hundred years of American architectural history.

Throughout the area, softening and coloring streetscapes, nestling quietly into a secluded side yard or climbing up a sunny hillside, lie the gardens. Some wear the patina of generations; others are recent in origin. Along with the architecture, the topography, and the ever-present ghosts of history, these gardens help to create that elusive quality we call "a sense of place."

Three officially designated historic districts—Twickenham (the name briefly imposed by town patriarch Leroy Pope on his rough-and-ready frontier settlement), Old Town, and Five Points—encompass much of the area today. Until the town burst its early boundaries after World War II, most of Huntsville's business and professional class lived here. To the north, south, and west radiated other long-time residential neighborhoods, home to the town's African-American population and most of the workers who toiled in the great cotton mills. Urban renewal would obliterate some of these neighborhoods in the 1960s; others still hang on today. But as part of Huntsville's "landscape of memory," they remain forever part of the city's history.

Formally recognizing historic neighborhoods is clearly desirable and beneficial. At the same time, it can be rather artificial. After all, the essence of community goes beyond a legally defined boundary and is certainly more profound than the trendy, self-conscious elitism which such designation can oftentimes breed. "Community" in the truest sense is a substantial part of the evolutionary human story itself.

That Huntsville has chosen to recognize its own wonderful historic neighborhoods and the sense of traditional community they express speaks well for the city's vision of its future. Such neighborhoods—with their mansions (or their mill houses), their places of worship, corner stores, porches, backyards and flower gardens, their memories of past lives, their sidewalks made for twilight strolls and friendly chance encounters—enhance the quality of civic life and ultimately nourish our own personal sensibilities. With lively text, lush photos, and engaging design, Donna Castellano, Charlie Seifried, and Betty Howard introduce us here to one lovely aspect of this community tapestry. May it open our eyes to others.

– Robert Gamble
Senior Architectural Historian
Alabama Historical Commission

Introduction

Gardens stir up in me a sense of awe. Like viewing any work of art, I am awed by the talent of people who possess the vision, the skill, and the genius to transform inert matter, the stuff of this earth, into something divine. But gardeners face another challenge; unlike the sculptor or painter, gardeners require the active cooperation of nature—its cycles, its processes, its miracles—to produce their art. They blend dirt and water and seeds and sun in a joyful mix that turns into a magical display of nature's bounty. Their work is more than a creation of art; it is the creation and perpetuation of life.

The gardens you will visit in this book are living works of art that grow behind some of the most spectacular and charming homes in Huntsville's historic districts. These gardens, along with many others in the districts, contribute to the texture of Huntsville's historic neighborhoods. But their distinctive setting is not the source of their beauty. The charm of these gardens, the art of these gardens, is the unique way each garden owner has combined materials universally available to us all, with things found, given, or discovered, and shaped their own masterpiece. Gracious all, these owners have opened their garden gates and invited us to come in to enjoy a private and treasured spot.

In addition to opening their gardens to us, the garden owners have also agreed to share with us stories of how their gardens grow. Through this, we see that these gardens are more than the artful compositions of their owners, but also the repository of some of their fondest and most personal memories: The rose bush around the arbor grew from a cutting taken by the owner's mother from the bush that grew in her grandmother's backyard; the boxwoods in the hedge were a gift from a treasured friend and have been moved and transplanted from four previous residences; the stones mounded carelessly beside a fountain were gathered on a favorite family vacation in France. Through these recollections, we have been invited to experience two gardens: the visible garden that we can see and experience through our senses and the secret garden that grows in the heart and through the memories of its creator. These gardens grow deep roots.

In the pages that follow, you will have the opportunity to visit these gardens and visit with the garden owners. As they tell about their gardens, some may dispense gardening advice, others may tell family stories, and others may share their philosophy of gardening. But, they have been looking forward to your visit and are so glad you could come.

– Donna McPherson Castellano

the Garden of
Bill Nance

An Unassuming Character

The front yard offers the first clue that an accomplished gardener resides in the 1920s bungalow on a street in downtown Huntsville. The postage-stamp-sized space is awash in color from flowers that thrive in the expertly designed beds that border the inviting stone walk. Passersby frequently stop and study this yard, hoping to glean ideas to use in their own gardens. Their eyes are led by the stone walk to a garden gate, sheltered by an archway of clematis and jessamine and decorated with a copper sunface whose expression is somewhat enigmatic. The garden beyond tempts them; they wonder at the vistas that must await those who pass through that door and enter this private garden.

A copper sunface created by Bill greets visitors who follow the impatiens-bordered path to his garden door.

A view through the garden from the pergola entry, past the pool, to a perfect circle of pink tulips teasing in the distance.

Summer brings a wash of white blooms around the pool as a melody of greens enriches the view.

Aside from the copper sunface on his garden door, there is nothing enigmatic about this garden's creator. Bill Nance wears his reputation casually, and his manner is as easy and inviting as a swimming hole on a hot day. Although he and his garden have been featured in several national magazines, his demeanor reflects his previous profession. At heart, Bill is still the artist and teacher. Always ready with encouraging words, he urges clients, students, and friends to follow their instincts and fill their gardens with the things they love.

Bill's garden accomplishes the impossible. On a small city lot, he has strung together three circular garden rooms that seem removed from place and time. These spaces entice you to sit and enjoy while luring you on to the next room to see the surprises that surely await. In the first garden, a bench offers a lovely spot to enjoy the splashing sound of the fishpond, but the herb garden in the middle room draws you forward with its delightful smells. A glimpse of a dramatic rooftop teases you on to the back garden, where the space opens up dramatically to reveal a charming summer house with a perfect circle of grass beckoning like a welcome mat.

Tea time in the gazebo.

The artful arrangement of the garden initially focuses your attention on the magical transition from garden room to garden room, but slowly the garden's intricate details come into view: Brick paths fade off into gravel walks, and flower beds and borders resemble the careless ease of a graceful flower arrangement. Views are constantly presented in new and intriguing ways.

The garden's air of abundance and casual graciousness originates in Bill's southern roots, but Bill is also a serious student of Chinese garden design and uses techniques found in Chinese and Japanese gardens to give the sense that you are in a much larger space. This is accomplished by creating multiple focal points that are viewed from a constantly changing perspective as you move through the space.

From the back porch, the summer house sits to the right. The lattice frames a perfect view.

In a garden filled with so many possibilities, one wonders which spot is Bill's favorite. Where does he go to drink his morning coffee or enjoy an evening glass of wine? When asked, Bill laughs: "I have no favorites among my children; I enjoy them all at the time they are meant to be enjoyed. I look at my tulips; when they turn brown, I've got something else to see. I have something to enjoy 365 days a year."

We should all be so lucky.

The view of Bill's front porch reveals distinctive lanterns from Istanbul.

A Paradise of Our Own Making

Entering the house for the first time, Lynn and her late
husband Harvie Jones sensed they had found the place
that would become their home. As they walked through
the house, they came to an expansive family room
whose wall of windows framed a view of a nondescript
backyard overgrown with ivy. Lynn did not see what
was there, but what *could be* there, and immediately
thought, "What a wonderful place for a garden." Since
that day, Lynn has worked to turn the backyard she
first glimpsed into the garden she envisioned.

Paradeisos: Greek; park, paradise,
of Persian origin: an enclosed garden.
An expression of man's search for a
private paradise.

The garden is divided by a stone-and-gravel
path which leads visitors to the stone wall and
a Celtic cross surrounded by pansies.

17

Tucked into an alcove, a pedestal topped with an armillary sundial is covered with clematis blooms.

Lynn found she had natural advantages and faced natural challenges as she fashioned her garden. Since the house and garden sit immediately at the base of a hill, the garden looked out to a gorgeous hillside view. An old, ivy-covered stone wall at the base of the hill contributed great natural character to the small space. The fence, which helped define the perimeter of the space, also blocked views into neighboring yards and heightened the feeling of an enclosed garden. But it was not all paradise. The hillside, which provided such a beautiful vista, also posed problems. It blocked almost all southern light, and the garden area was poorly drained. Equally confounding was the red clay soil and a southern heat that wilted all but the most resilient plants.

Lynn credits the success of her garden to her decision to use plants able to withstand Alabama's hot summers. However, she ruefully acknowledges, this decision came after much work and frustration on her part. Lynn's journey as a gardener began with her willingness to educate herself. She took a Master Gardener class, poured over gardening books, and traveled to famous gardens—all the while developing an eye for what she loved. Lynn credits trips to English gardens with fueling her "English garden phase"—when she tried to create a garden of perennials more at home in Vita Sackville-West's Sissinghurst than in Huntsville. Frustration associated with this experiment led Lynn to forego a garden of ever-changing perennials and embrace plants that would thrive in their natural environment.

Sounds of bubbling water provide
a serene backdrop.

Lynn admits that one of the joys of her garden is
that the work will never be complete. Her garden is
not a static composition but a space that is constantly
evolving. She recalls the notion of a garden as a
paradeisos—a space that is not only beautiful but
a source of meditation and contemplation for its
owner. Lynn's *paradeisos* is a place for enjoying
early morning coffee and the newspaper, where
visiting family and friends congregate for simple
meals, a glass of wine, good conversation. It is a
place of inspiration, work, pride, and enjoyment.
And it is where she can watch the birds, taking
their baths in the fountain, raise their families in
the place she created. It is a place that reminds us
each make our own paradise—and every moment
spent creating it is a memory to be savored.

Japanese red maples contrast with cherry
tree blossoms and azalea blooms to create
a symphony of pink.

In Her Natural Environment

An observer of happenings on Adams Street would, after time, notice an unusual pattern of behavior. Regardless of the side of the street they were on or the pace they had set, joggers, walkers, bicyclers, all tend to slow down and cross the street to travel past the low rock wall that runs along the sidewalk in front of the gracious antebellum home. What draws the attention of passersby is the collection of Alabama native plants and wildflowers, tucked like tiny treasures, growing in the rock crevices and along the base of the wall.

This vista is the work of Claire Johnston, whose love of Alabama's environment led her to create a scene you might encounter on a walk in the woods, where moss, ferns, and the delicate ephemerals of spring create their own compositions guided only by the hand of nature.

A stately old dogwood has shaded generations who have gathered at the antebellum home.

This wall is symbolic of Claire's love of native plants and her approach to garden design: Let nature, in all its simplicity, be your guide.

To fully appreciate the gardens that surround this welcoming house, you must first understand its owner and her love of a natural environment. In a previous residence, Claire created a garden that was akin to a rescue mission made up of plants she transplanted from areas threatened by new development. These efforts were not carried out in a haphazard way; Claire became a student of Alabama's native plants, reading and studying extensively, to know which plants could be transplanted without harm. When she and her husband Bill decided to move into the house on Adams, she created a garden that reflected her love of natural surroundings. The wall immediately caught Claire's attention. It is such a natural structure, she explains, that she could never imagine anything other than a natural treatment for the space. She envisioned the wall planted with wild flowers, and it was the perfect start to her garden.

A view of the garden from one of the comfortable back porches.

...moss, ferns, and the delicate ephemerals of spring create their own compositions guided only by the hand of nature.

Her natural, uncomplicated approach to garden design continues throughout the garden. In the sweeping beds around the expansive property, simplicity reigns — color is understated, structure is uncomplicated, and the curving, graceful lines of the garden create a very welcoming effect. Filling out the beds and lawn are threatened plants and trees she rescued and brought with her from her previous residence. These flowering trees and berried shrubs, along with the showy blossoms of lace cap, annabelle, and french hydrangeas, fill in the beds that surround portions of the house and hug the stone walls. Claire points out that the back garden is still very much a work-in-progress. She and her husband Bill have lived in the house for only about four years, but the structure of what will develop is clearly visible.

Although the garden invites visitors to explore, Claire confides that the best views of the garden are from the house. Her favorite view is from the conservatory, where she can sit and observe the entire garden, noting which plants are coming up and which are ready to bloom. The spacious, comfortable porches that hug the rear of the house offer beautiful views as well. Here, a visitor is likely to be joined by Claire's dogs BJ and Lucky, two loveable mutts rescued by Claire. Adding to the charm of the porch are the simple, understated furnishings, many of which were favorite childhood pieces.

Drawn to simplicity, Claire explains that she did not choose the things that fill her house for their grandness or pedigree. Everything here, she quietly states, is here because she loves it. Cherished pieces may or may not be grand antiques, but like the ephemerals that grow along the front wall, they all have a place with Claire.

A favorite view from the conservatory.

Our English Sabbatical

A number of years ago, Bill Munson, a
professor of English literature, spent six
months researching medieval texts at the
Bodleian Library at Oxford University,
just north of London. He lived the life
of a scholar: He rose, ate breakfast, and
walked the few blocks to the library where,
poring over illuminated manuscripts, he
entered 14th-century England through
the works of Geoffrey Chaucer.

As Bill toiled away within the hallowed
walls of academia, Nancy, his wife of more
than 40 years, pursued research interests
of her own. A serious gardener, Nancy
wanted to discover as much as she could
about the design and history of English
gardens. While this task required some
library time, most of the work could be

The walls and roof of this pergola are
engulfed with roses in early May.

The Munsons' enclosed porch offers shaded comfort.

Herbs grow in beds at the center of the fenced garden.

carried out visiting the historic gardens around Blenheim Palace, walking through gardens in the villages of Chipping Camden, Bourton-on-the-Water, and Steeple Aston, or on weekend trips with Bill to Vita Sackville-West's Sissinghurst or Rosemary Verey's Barnsley. Her research findings were not published in a scholarly journal but can be seen in the backyard where Nancy created a garden inspired by their sabbatical together in England.

The glory of this garden is in early May, when the blooms of Nancy's heirloom climbing roses overwhelm the English mix of perennial and shrub borders with soft color and heady scent. Nancy's garden is divided into three distinct spaces. Located closest to the house is an herb garden enclosed with a wrought iron fence found by Bill at an antique shop. Thyme, rosemary, and other herbs grow in beds at its center, and perennials clustered next to the fence provide an infusion of color. Climbing roses grow at the sides and along the top of the fence. For a few weeks in May, the small garden is encased within a soft wall of roses. Nancy confides that she thinks this is Bill's favorite time in this space—when he retreats to a bench and imagines that he is in a cloister garden.

Spring perennials provide an infusion of color.

The herb garden opens to a middle garden with a broad lawn of grass bordered by beds containing specimen trees, flowering shrubs, and perennials. Nancy estimates her garden contains more than 250 species of plants, shrubs, and trees. The focal point of the middle garden is a lattice arbor Nancy designed. The arbor is planted with *Rosa moschata plena,* an antique species rose that is similar, if not identical to, the rose Vita Sackville-West used on the white garden arbor at Sissinghurst.

As visitors enter the back garden through the arbor, they see another patch of grass bordered by raised beds of flowering shrubs and perennials. Placed in its center is a bench swing in a pergola. The walls and roof provide a wonderful climbing surface for the roses around it, and the small structure is engulfed by rose blossoms in early May.

Before the unforgiving heat of an Alabama summer over-powers the flowers in the abundant beds, this garden pays proper homage to the land of its inspiration. The garden is a great reminder of their experience together. The enclosed herb garden, symbolically a place of contemplation, provides a retreat for quiet musings. Nancy's blooming roses and perennial beds create an English garden that is a delight for the senses. This garden provides a place for the mind as well as the senses, and Nancy has created a happy marriage between the two.

A view from one garden to the next, where a pergola and swing
are overtaken by a rush of spring rose blossoms.

the Garden of
Randy Roper

The Sorcerer's Tale

Nestled behind a quiet bungalow grows an understated, evergreen garden with a chameleon-like ability to become suddenly grand with the addition of a few carefully chosen accessories. It helps, of course, when the individual aiding the transformation is Randy Roper, the home's owner and noted Huntsville designer, whose impeccable taste and unerring eye are exceeded only by his biting wit—all of which are exercised with great aplomb. By creating a formal garden with a color palette restricted to varying shades of green and white, Randy fashions a place where his design wizardry can operate with few restrictions.

This jewel of a garden had humble beginnings. When Randy bought the property in 1978, the backyard contained massive amounts of bamboo, a hackberry tree, and a small garage. The first year or so he owned the property he made a few changes. Randy and his dad pulled up and hauled away truckloads of bamboo, and he converted the garage into a small guest house.

The clean, simple lines of this garden allow Randy
to create a new look at a moment's notice.

By creating a formal garden with a color palette restricted to varying shades of green and white, Randy fashions a place where his design wizardry can operate with few restrictions.

Major changes came years later, when, in 1994 after completing an addition to the back of the bungalow, he tore down the guest house to gain more space in his back yard. This increased the size of the garden, and provided a delightful borrowed view, as his garden now overlooked the expansive backyard of an adjacent property. To keep an airy, open feel to the small garden, Randy designed the pergola to mirror the back façade of his home, thereby unifying the space. He limited his plants to a proven few—boxwoods, acuba, oak leaf hydrangeas, and azaleas. The garden's simplicity created a neutral backdrop whose appearance could be changed at any time. Colorful china, a floral arrangement, and table-cloth at the gazebo, bright pillows on the sofa and chairs, blooming flowers in pots—all are tools Randy can use when he wants his garden to have a different look.

A captivating composition of white spirea, magenta azaleas, and a 19th-century statue.

The pergola, set for a simple luncheon, with a borrowed
view of a neighbor's property in the distance.

Since rules were made to be broken, the exception to the green-and-white palette is found along the side garden. Under an archway of white spirea, a 19th-century Italian statue rests in a mound of magenta azaleas, whose brilliant burst of color announces spring to the neighborhood.

In this very refined space, the only touch of whimsy is the bird feeder perched on the fence with a cat ready to pounce. This hints at the owner's irreverent sense of humor but also pays homage to one of Adams Street's most legendary residents, Randy's cat Winston. Winston ruled Adams with the quiet authority that can only be exercised by a cat, who, in return,

received the patient indulgence of all neighborhood residents. According to legend, one day an irate neighbor phoned Randy to complain about Winston. She accused the cat of sneaking into her house and stealing a ham from the kitchen. As Randy assured the neighbor she must be mistaken, he looked out to see Winston dragging a ham down the driveway.

By designing a formal space with a restrained color palette, Randy can conjure a garden capable of many moods. It can be a stunning setting for a formal dinner party, a dressed down space for a casual evening with friends, or the hunting grounds of a favorite cat. And accomplish all with equal aplomb.

the Garden of
Kay and Don Wheeler

A Time to Play

Houses and front gardens have their own personalities. Some houses and front gardens have a reserved and formal attitude while others show a convivial and playful disposition. This friendly white cottage, with a profusion of white tulips and pansies to herald spring, has an optimistic, cheerful spirit—a spirit shared with its owners, Kay and Don Wheeler. This house cast its spell on Kay the first time she saw it, but she waited 20 years for the opportunity to own it—proving, yet again, that some things are worth the wait. Married for more than 42 years, Don and Kay have an easy warmth and affection for one another. They, and their house, are filled with laughter and good humor—and all who enter its domain are touched by its warmth and hospitality.

Practical considerations determined the layout of this garden. The house backs up to a steep lot, and the previous owners had solved the problem of the sloping lot by building a series of multi-tiered terraces.

A billowing American flag waves visitors to the cheerful entrance of the Wheeler home.

The side garden with arched entry functions as a foyer for visitors entering from the front yard.

Since Don and Kay wanted to add a garage—which would tear this landscaping system apart—they had to find another solution. The house needed work, and Kay took responsibility for the home's interior and assigned Don to fix the backyard. On the advice of a friend, Don decided to divide the yard into two sections so that the garden would consist of an upper and lower level, and connect them with a stone wall and steps. To create a sense of expansiveness and prevent the yard from seeming chopped up, they would unify the space with a grassy lawn—which also flows down and surrounds the flagstone terrace and screened back porch, integrating the spaces together.

Kay left the backyard in good hands. Don's childhood prepared him well for the task: He grew up on a farm and credits those early years for

his love of "working in the dirt." He continued his affiliation with dirt, growing a small vegetable garden during medical internship in Memphis. After settling in Huntsville, Don became quite serious about roses and grew and maintained a beautiful rose garden, until, as he says, "the Japanese beetles put me out of business." For the space behind this new house, he wanted a garden with easy plants that required minimal attention — preferring to spend his time doting on grandchildren rather than fussing over a flower bed.

The garden's structure is created by crepe myrtles, boxwoods, and azaleas, with hostas and hydrangeas adding texture and color in spring and summer. The side garden with arched entry functions as a foyer for visitors entering from the front yard. What began as Kay's cutting garden runs along one side, but lack of light — and Don says too much work — called for a change of plans. Azaleas will grace the area until, they both agree, something better suggests itself. To add a bit of the unexpected to the garden, Don plants the crevices in the stone steps and brick walls with white pansies and impatiens. This graceful touch leads visitors' eyes up the stone steps and to the swing at the garden's far edge. At night, the moonlight reflected off their white blooms gives the garden a luminescent glow.

Don insists that every garden should have a secret place — a little hideway where one can run away and play, sight unseen. This garden's secret place is in the back corner, behind the little guest house. This spot will be irresistible to grandchildren playing their games of hide-and-seek, or telling stories, or stealing away with a sandwich and cookies for an impromptu picnic. No doubt, they will be joined by their grandparents — two people who remain young in spirit — who, like their grandchildren, can't resist the opportunity to play.

The Wheelers' expansive back garden offers many places for playful encounters with their grandchildren.

the Garden of
Virginia and Parker Griffith

Art by Subtraction

Some spaces call out for gardens that are
flights of fancy and imagination, where a
mad mix of blooming flowers and flowing
fountains creates a garden that is an adven-
ture in itself. And then there are spaces
where one treads lightly. Places where
history and architecture intersect, and the
challenge of a garden owner is to fashion
a space that complements, not competes
with, an original structure. Creating a garden
to surround the 1824 home designed and
built by Huntsville architect George Steele
called for a design that echoed the strong
architectural presence of the residence
without overshadowing its understated
elegance. Under the sure hand of Virginia
and Parker Griffith, this Randolph Avenue
landmark is enhanced by a garden whose
clean, sculptural lines provide a modern
interpretation of the architectural vision
of George Steele.

The Griffiths' understated view of history.

The lines of the lower garden illustrate Virginia's sculptural approach to gardening.

The refined design of the garden reflects the artistic sensibilities of Virginia Griffith. Watching the work of stonemasons on a television program about the restoration of cathedrals, Virginia was inspired to learn to sculpt. At first, Virginia dismissed the notion, but her husband Parker urged her to pursue the idea —and she did. Through sculpting, Virginia learned about "art by subtraction," the theory that sculptors create their art by chipping away stone and gradually revealing the figure that is hidden within. This principle has guided Virginia in whatever she creates—whether chiseling away at stone or refining and editing a garden, placing its classic, pared-down elegance on display.

Virginia points out that she inherited a garden with beautiful bones, but she wanted to modify the space to suit her family's needs. The garden consists of two tiers, an upper and lower tier, divided by a hedge with a vine-covered arch. Initially, there was a swimming pool in the upper tier and a gazebo and oval pad of grass bounded by the brick walkway in the lower tier. Virginia removed the swimming pool, increasing the size of the lawn, and added a patio on the far side of the yard. Shutters installed along the side wall create a distinctive architectural feature and add to the sense of privacy in the area. Further, Virginia proudly points out, the patio was laid with bricks recycled from the basement of the 1824 house. Since Steele owned several brick factories, it is likely the old bricks in the patio were made in one of his factories.

Pink azaleas and a Japanese maple provide a whisper of spring color.

Virginia uses evergreen hedges, primarily boxwoods and azaleas, to define the garden's shape. Aside from a burst of early pink azaleas and the dramatic deep red of a Japanese maple, the colors in this garden are limited to varying shades of green punctuated with the white blooms of dogwood trees. The side garden, running parallel to the house and adjoining a downtown street, is one of the most recognized gardens in Huntsville. Again, in this structured, formal space, simplicity rules as Virginia uses

evergreen boxwoods and azaleas to define the garden's shape and softens its edges with verdant ferns, variegated hostas, and mondo grass.

It takes a talented artist with a discerning eye to interpret the difference between simple elegance and cold austerity. This garden is a study in restraint and subtlety, and beautifully illustrates the principle that some of the most powerful statements are those that are whispered.

This side garden is one of the most recognized gardens in Huntsville.

*Any town that doesn't have
sidewalks doesn't love its children.*

– Margaret Mead

As the setting sun signals the day's end, we
find a young family on a walk, taking part
in a nightly ritual shared by many residents
in our neighborhoods.

Our neighborhood sidewalks are the stage upon
which many human dramas are performed.
This is where we laugh over a day's adventures,
commiserate over a day's disappointments, or
offer advice, solace, and a sympathetic ear to
friends as they pour out their hearts.

A sidewalk is a concrete path etched with
memories. On its surface, down our streets,
near our gardens, bonds of family and friend-
ship are formed and affirmed. Ideas are born
and plans are made.

A sidewalk is a place of promise, of possibilities.

Take a walk and discover its magic.

A Full Circle

The garden created by Ann and Bruce Garnett is, quite simply, their life's work. A couple who found one another later in life, each pursued their love of gardening separately until fate brought them together. They married, appropriately enough, in the spring of 1995 in a garden created by Ann. A brilliant collaboration began with the joining of their spirits. The home and garden they created became a space that reflected both their love for one another and their passion for gardening.

Trips to the south of France or Nantucket became an opportunity for them to scour local gardens and shops and find ideas to bring back with them. For Ann and Bruce, entering their garden was not just a visual delight, but a walk down memory lane — as their time together was represented symbolically within this special place.

This allee of crepe myrtles forms a dramatic entry to the garden.

Pan dances atop a mound of green-and-white caladiums. The "Blue Door to Nowhere" was inspired by a favorite trip to Nice.

Ann credits a horticultural class taken at LSU with awakening her to the joys of gardening. Studying the propagation of plants—learning how to graft or root cuttings—she became aware of what she calls "the wonderful miracle of life." After moving to Huntsville, she became involved with other "miracles of life"—the raising of three children that limited her garden projects to basic maintenance and upkeep.

Latticed columns flanking the Lutyens bench
recall a vacation in Nantucket.

This garden is a place of warmth, a place of renewal. It holds the sure promise
that there is life in the bulb just waiting to burst out with the first call of spring.

As her children grew older, Ann had an opportunity to become, as she puts it, "a true gardener." She developed an awareness of garden design, but also became attentive to plants in their environments—why some thrived, why some did okay, and why some died. She learned how to play in her garden—to dig and transplant and experiment, to move things around and see how certain plants looked with one another. And she learned that she loved to nurture little cuttings and watch them grow into strong, thriving plants.

As Ann made these discoveries, Bruce followed a similar path. A successful career in the Army sent him all over the world, and gardening became a way for Bruce to adjust to life in a new place—to put down roots. The drawback was that he never lived in one place long enough to see what he had planted grow.

Their garden became a place where they could work together, play together, and where, together, they could watch what they planted grow. It is entered through a distinctive garden gate that opens into a dramatic allee of crepe myrtles. The focal point from the entry is a dancing figure of Pan, sheltered by a sweetbay magnolia encircled by boxwoods and white caladiums. The shadow cast by the magnolia provides a shaded patio area for entertaining. Two large ferns mark the entrance to the heart of the garden, defined by a grassy circle bordered with stepping stones. A trip to Nantucket provided the inspiration for the two latticed columns that flank the weathered Lutyens bench, and the "Blue Door to Nowhere" recalls a favorite trip to the South of France. Ann volunteers that the door was painted twenty different times to find the right shade of blue. The fountain tucked in the corner holds memories of France—the rocks piled around

A renowned cook, Ann has easy access to her herb garden located beside the kitchen door.

the pool were collected on a beach in Nice. Swimming in the pond are goldfish—one for each of their seven grandchildren. The gallery that runs along the side of the garage provides a quiet place to sit and view the garden.

Ann and Bruce planted deep roots in this garden. Ann points out with pride that she grew the hydrangeas and acuba in the garden from her cuttings. Other flowers and bushes were also started from cuttings brought from their frequent travels. Ann laughs that they always travelled with Ziploc bags, duct tape, and clippers. Because she marvels at how bulbs and seeds produce life, she collects caladium bulbs every fall to replant in the spring. She asks, "How can anyone throw away something that's still living?"

For eight years, this garden flourished under the tender love and care provided by Ann and Bruce. Now, their garden returns the favor. Bruce's unexpected death left Ann to tend the garden by herself. This garden is a constant memory of Bruce's spirit and of the life they created together. It is a place of warmth, a place of renewal. It holds the sure promise that there is life in the bulb just waiting to burst out with the first call of spring.

■

the Garden of
Kathleen and Philip Dotts

Beholding Beauty

A May visit to the garden of Philip and Kathleen Dotts brings an invitation to see Shakespeare's Sweet Juliet, Othello, and Falstaff or Chaucer's Wife of Bath, Knight, or Yeoman from *The Canterbury Tales*. Lest you think Kathleen, an English literature teacher, has crossed the line separating reality from fantasy, you should know that these characters are names of roses blooming in Kathleen's garden. Creating a rose garden composed of heirloom roses named after famous literary or historical figures allowed her to combine her passion for history and literature with her love of old-fashioned roses. Here, behind the blue clapboard Victorian house with the white gingerbread trim, it is quite possible to have tea with Cordelia or share a glass of wine with the Prince in a garden fragrant with the smell of rose blossoms.

The breathtaking view of a rose garden seen today is not the vision that greeted Philip and Kathleen when they first purchased this house in 1980. There was no grass and the backyard was open to a busy four-lane thoroughfare. A major renovation several years later added the back porch and second-floor sleeping porch, and the outline of the garden that exists today began beneath the sheltering arm of the dogwood tree. Enclosed in two concentric circles of broken, moss-covered

The garden is filled with fragrant heirloom roses whose names bear a historical or literary significance.

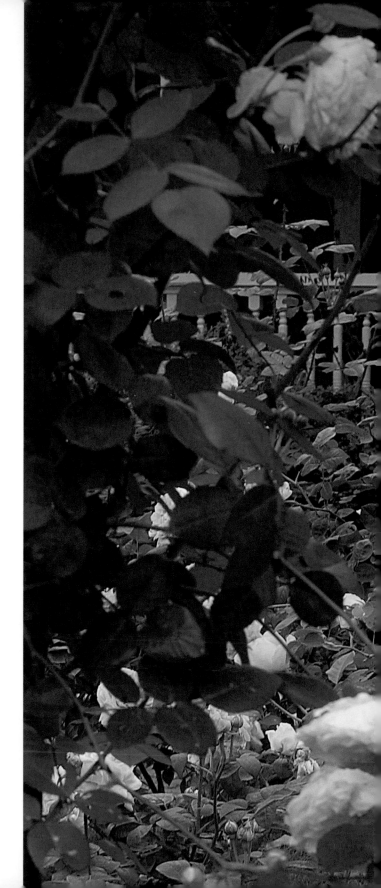

Kathleen notes that imperfection surrounds us and will always be a part of us. Our challenge, she insists, is to appreciate beauty whenever we can — in all its forms, wherever it appears — because it is always fleeting.

stone is a fountain, surrounded by smooth river rocks, and breathtaking from either the balcony or down the stone path along the side of the house. The addition of a pergola to an old barn that sat at the back of the property, coupled with the installation of architecturally salvaged doors from a southwestern monastery, turned an old eyesore into a commanding focal point. The backyard still served double duty as a gathering place for kids—a trampoline occupied center court—and a place where Kathleen read and graded papers to the sounds of laughing children.

The idea for her present rose garden took shape while planning the festivities for their twenty-fifth wedding anniversary. Kathleen had always had roses in her garden, but she wanted more. She wanted a garden filled with roses. Overtaken with roses. And not just any roses, but fragrant, heirloom roses—roses whose soft, sweet scent would be carried by breezes to the porch or lifted up to the balcony. And, she wanted roses whose names bore a historical or literary significance. A garden with the Prince

The fountain, encircled by moss-covered rock and stone, is sheltered under the branch of a dogwood tree.

A formal rock-and-stone path leads to the pergola bursting with rose blooms.

and Falstaff should also have the Red Rose of Lancaster or the White Rose of York—the dueling families during England's War of the Roses. Kathleen found a place for Teddy Roosevelt —as well as roses whose names hint at a rich story. One of Kathleen's favorites is Maiden's Blush, a pink rose whose pale, outer leaves deepen to crimson in the center. Kathleen points out that, in France, the translated name of the same rose is the Thigh of the Passionate Nymph, proving once again, Kathleen suggests with a wink, that significant differences separate English and French culture.

Kathleen's devotion to her heirloom rose garden reflects a unique perspective on life. The challenges of growing roses in an inhospitable climate do not deter her, nor does she surrender

in the face of Japanese beetles, powdery mildew, and black spot. She is not saddened when the first magnificent blush of roses fades into a sporadic blooming season that finally leaves her garden bare. Kathleen insists she never questions the trials of growing roses—any more than she questions whether a child's imperfection tests a parent's love. She points out that imperfection surrounds us and will always be a part of us. Our challenge, she insists, is to appreciate beauty whenever we can—in all its forms, wherever it appears—because it is always fleeting.

Stop by Kathleen's rose garden one May morning. Walk around, smell the blossoms, and behold beauty—in all its fleeting glory.

A sidewalk bouquet of larkspur, nasturtium, and snapdragons.

Coloring Outside the Lines

Some gardens, like their owner's personalities, are just too expansive to stay confined within a small area. They spill over their boundaries, touching all they encounter with their ebullience, drawing more and more people into an ever-expanding circle of friends. The front garden of this bungalow with the blue front porch has such a presence, matching the youthful spirit of its residents, Brimmer and Stephanie Sherman and their young daughter, Brooke.

Originally from Santa Fe, New Mexico, Stephanie adds a southwestern twist to the way her neighborhood practices southern hospitality. Fitting a family of three comfortably in a bungalow requires that every inch of the house be used. A porch is not treated as a decorative façade, but as another room ready for use. Several years ago, when hosting a birthday celebration for Brimmer, Stephanie decided to move the festivities to the porch so guests would have more room. Neighbors walking down the

Stephanie's decorative flourishes create a festive setting for a neighborhood party as the Shermans' porch becomes an extension of their living area.

street called their birthday greetings to Brimmer, and Stephanie responded by inviting them to "come on up and join the party." This party became the genesis of her famous potluck suppers. Neighbors gather on the porch — always festively decked out for the occasion — and bring their signature dishes to share with friends while everyone catches up over margaritas.

Stephanie's version of southern hospitality does not stop at the porch — nor does she relegate her garden to the backyard or confine it to beds planted along the front of the house.

Stephanie adopted the strip of land between the sidewalk and the street and planted a sidewalk garden, where blooms of larkspur, nasturtium, sedum, and helleborus spill over and form a casual summer bouquet for the street.

In this neighborhood where sidewalks abound and friends walk down the block to visit, the flowers Stephanie shares in her sidewalk garden makes everyone's journey more pleasant. Her gift reminds us that gardens, like friendships, can grow in the most unlikely of places — as long as they're lovingly tended.

the Garden of
Vivian Martin

A Childhood Dream

Let's pretend we're five years old. It is our
birthday, and our parents have promised
a very special present. We spend the day
waiting for its arrival, peppering our mom
with questions of what it is and when it will
get here with the untiring dedication only a
young child can muster. Finally, we hear a
commotion on the street. We look out to see
a playhouse, a beautiful yellow playhouse,
on a forklift truck making its way down our
driveway. Our mother looks at us and says,
"Here is a little house just for you." This
is the stuff dreams are made of.

When Vivian and Frederick Martin gave
their young daughter Lucinda this playhouse many years ago, they gave a gift that,
in turn, provided their family with lasting
childhood memories.

A porch as glorious as this, with such profuse
color, is reminiscent of an Impressionist painting.

Set for a tea party, this playhouse has been a favorite retreat for generations of Martin children.

The playhouse became a favorite spot of the three Martin children for tea parties, birthday parties, Cub Scout meetings—and offered a quiet sanctuary to daydream or read a book. When Vivian moved from the family home several years ago, the playhouse— like other beloved family possessions—made the trip as well. Now, it sits in her backyard, a place where old memories dwell and fresh memories are made as younger generations of Martin children claim the house for their own.

The playhouse, the focus of so much childhood activity, is now the centerpiece of Vivian's garden. The garden's shape is defined by an oval grass lawn, with the residence at one end and the playhouse situated diagonally opposite. The grass lawn is bordered by a curving walkway made from old moss-covered stone, inset with three millstones brought from her former home. The walkway continues past the playhouse, where massed plantings of inky-blue hydrangeas and crepe myrtles complete the oval shape. Just beyond the playhouse is a short path that connects Vivian's yard to her daughter Lucinda's. This path became the favored mode of transportation for Vivian's grandchildren and their playmates as they slipped back and forth between the two yards.

Looking out from her sun room, or the kitchen, or the screened back porch, Vivian enjoys a perfect view of her garden. From this vantage point, she can see the garden below her and recall a period of her children's youth—when laughter and shouts from games of Cowboys and Indians filled the backyard, and pots of make-believe tea poured into dainty teacups. Embedded in her garden are memories—and the sure knowledge that the playhouse she and Frederick gave to their daughter on that day so many years ago continues to bring "many happy returns" to her family.

A view of Vivian's house from the playhouse. The grass lawn bordered with moss-covered stone comes to life with a lively display of impatiens and hydrangeas.

The easygoing appearance of the house and garden reflect Rusty's laid-back attitude.

The Cows Have Come Home

The charm of some gardens—and some people, too—is that they do not take themselves too seriously. Rusty George has such a garden—insisting the space behind his Five Points house is a yard, not a garden. No matter. Rusty's garden offers a lighthearted peek into the good-natured, fun-loving, slightly eccentric side of some of the people who live in our historic districts. One month a year, Rusty's garden is visited by Lily and Flagg.

The two life-sized cows were named after Huntsville's world-famous dairy cow Lily Flagg, recognized at the 1892 Chicago World's Fair as the world's greatest butterfat producer. Lily and Flagg

Lily and Flagg enjoying a sunny summer day.

were adopted by a group of concerned residents after they were, quite literally, put on the street several years ago during a local furniture store's going-out-of-business sale. Since the opportunity to own livestock does not come along every day, the band of friends decided to pool their money, purchase the cows, and draw straws to determine who gets "grazing privileges" each month. We caught up with Lily and Flagg sampling grass in Rusty's garden on a pretty June day—their heads not turned a bit by the attention they received. But, then again, that's just part of their charm.

Views of the neighborhood are an added benefit of
lunch on the Benzenhafers' front porch.

the Garden of
Cristina and Eric Benzenhafer

An iron fence surrounds the corner
garden off the end of the porch.

A Little Street Music

Many of us retreat to our gardens to escape from the hustle and bustle of our daily lives. Our gardens are places to pursue our "spirit and our solitude" and provide inspiration for periods of reflection and private contemplation. These are places where the sound of water bubbling in a fountain provides background music to coax thoughts and provoke intimate conversations.

Let's get real. Many district gardens are not secluded, private areas, but niches carved from spaces that may sit in full view of the world. As the garden of Cristina and Eric Benzenhafer shows, this perceived liability can add to a garden's charm. Downtown gardens do not have to be secluded, but can be a part of the landscape, part of the vista of the neighborhood. Rather than a place to retire from human contact, a front garden can foster interaction and provide a view of an endlessly changing street scene. Sounds made by the smacking of walking shoes or chatter of walkers and joggers form their own rhythmic sounds and remind us we are part of an active, vibrant community.

With a garden perched at the edge of an intersection, you are never alone. With a glass of tea and a comfortable chair, you can sit back and enjoy the constantly changing parade of passersby. Chances are, before long, you'll see a friend — or make a new one.

A corner garden offers Cristina and Eric
the chance to hide in plain view.

the Garden of
Nell and David Johnston

A Simple Pleasure

She had to be coaxed into even looking at
the house. Situated at the intersection of two
downtown streets, the yard had no privacy,
the house looked dark and uninviting,
the kitchen was all wrong, and in 1987,
Twickenham was not a sure bet in real
estate. Still, it was an architectural gem filled
with Huntsville history—and the staircase.
There was a grand, soaring staircase in
the entrance foyer that foreshadowed the
elegance found throughout the residence.
After a week or two of deliberation, they
bought the house. Since then, the kitchen
has been remodeled, the house has been
repainted, the staircase—still grand—also
doubles as a stage for the annual Christmas
pageants performed by their grandchildren.
The house now reflects the warmth and
graciousness of its owners, David and Nell
Johnston, who love to open their home to
family and friends.

A shady moss-covered walk and blooming hostas
lead to the sunny garden room in the distance.

The keyhole garden offers an intimate setting.

The yard, a small space that wraps around the back and side of the house, has been transformed into an intimate garden that is both a quiet retreat for David and Nell and a perfect setting for parties the couple enjoy hosting.

The secret to this garden resides in the ability of David and Nell to make the most of what they have. The space taken up by the residence, a porte cochere, and a carriage house left little area for an expansive garden. This liability became their inspiration, as they turned a series of oddly shaped open spaces into a garden made up of several captivating "garden rooms" connected by a moss-covered path. The walls of the residence and carriage house outline the perimeter of the garden, and hemlocks, crepe myrtles, hydrangeas, and rhododendrons define the rooms created within the garden's structure. There is a coyness to this garden, with views that do not flow unobstructed from one room to the next, but give just a glimpse of what lies down the path, drawing a visitor through, creating an air of mystery and the illusion that the garden is larger than it is.

The keyhole garden, whose curving boxwood walls provide a lush, protective barrier from the busy street just a few feet away, sets the tone for this garden experience. Surrounded by soft, green walls, this side garden is a private, intimate space and the perfect place for a small gathering with friends. Visitors are drawn from this room down a mossy path, which leads to a fountain and the soft sounds of gurgling water. A seating area situated under the arch of the conservatory offers a beautiful spot to view a tiered fountain. The path continues along to the side garden where, sheltered by hemlocks, the cool blue blooms of hydrangeas and inviting seating areas beg visitors to pause awhile. Here—whether you look back to the fountain, toward the lacy, arched gate, or directly ahead into the conservatory—is a view that is beautiful in all directions.

A secluded bench under the arch of the conservatory offers a view of the tiered fountain.

Here — whether you look back to the fountain, toward the lacy, arched gate, or directly ahead into the conservatory — is a view that is beautiful in all directions.

On one side of the iron gate, the path leads to a circle of chartreuse lily leaves and a tiered evergreen. On the other side, pink and blue hydrangeas nod toward the fountain.

Nell takes her garden seriously, but she is not a serious gardener. She does not keep copious notes about which plants were planted where or what variety of flower blooms best in a certain location. Because the garden's structure is so well-defined with evergreen shrubs and trees, all that's left for Nell is to accessorize with statuary, plants, pots, and flowers. Nell counts on her hydrangeas, crepe myrtles, and rhododendrons to provide her garden with colorful blooms, but, for the most part, Nell likes to fill in the rest of her garden with plants that appeal to her during visits to local nurseries. She admits this approach is unplanned—frankly, it's part of the appeal for her—because it gives her the freedom to choose plants that strike her fancy. David teases that the way he knows spring has arrived is when Nell pulls up with boxes and boxes of flowers streaming from the trunk and backseat of her car.

For David and Nell, their garden is not something that requires a great deal of work or is a source of stress. It is, quite frankly, a place they enjoy—their family, their friends, and themselves. Sometimes, a garden is just a simple pleasure.

With dramatic views of the surrounding garden, the glass walls and
high ceilings of the conservatory bring the outdoors inside.

the Garden of
Betsy and Peter Lowe

In the Heart of History

The residence situated in the triangular space between
Echols Avenue and McClung Avenue presides majestically
from the top of a hill. Here, surrounded by the sweeping,
terraced lawn that flows past the fountain and down to the
street, sits a house that has been a symbol of Huntsville
history for almost 200 years. Built on land owned by Leroy
Pope, one of Huntsville's founding fathers, the house stayed
in the Pope family for more than fifty years, eventually
becoming the home of LeRoy Pope Walker, the first
Secretary of War of the Confederacy.

For present residents, Betsy and Peter Lowe, ownership
of this house confers a special obligation. Not only do they
accept the responsibility to preserve this piece of Huntsville
history for future generations but they generously share
their landmark residence by hosting countless civic and
social functions for their community. Over the years, this
great house has been the setting for events attended by
many important historic figures. But it is also a home —
and it is in the home created by Betsy and Peter that the
Lowe children and grandchildren gather to celebrate and
affirm the bonds of family.

Possessing a garden that bore the imprint of history, the Lowes had the challenge of integrating the individual features of their garden into a fully coherent design.

In spite of a grand pedigree, the house experienced hard times. Divided into apartments by a previous owner, the house was brought back to its original grand elegance in a 1970s restoration. When Betsy and Peter bought the house in 1987, they continued the work of restoring the residence and grounds. Aside from the front lawn that provided a dramatic backdrop for the house, the grounds contained historically significant features. The pool at the bottom of the hill was the old City Reservoir, and water pumped here from Big Spring flowed through pipes to hydrants downtown. Possessing a garden that bore the imprint of history, the Lowes had the challenge of integrating the individual features of their garden into a fully coherent design. Betsy introduced structure to the space, and blurred the lines with gentle terraces and mass plantings of sweeping hydrangeas and a fragile rose garden so that the garden's formality is diffused by a blousy, feminine overlay.

Sweeping hydrangeas and curved walkways
soften the garden's formality.

A view into the home's stunning conservatory.

The formal, angular lines of the Greek Revival home are softened by the gentle sloping terraces which form the approach to the house. Betsy and Peter restored the old City Reservoir located at the base of the property into a beautiful pool inlaid with Italian tile. The pool and its statue form the centerpiece of the lower garden. Betsy's unabashed love of hydrangeas led her to plant the Nikko blue hydrangeas that provide a splash of color and echo the curving lines of the fountain and surrounding walkway. Visitors continuing up the steps to the house encounter the rose garden, whose blooms peer over an evergreen hedge and nod a gentle greeting. The entrance to the rose garden is marked by more hydrangeas, and a pad of green grass, cultivated into a notched rectangle, introduces geometric purity to the space. Boxwoods outline the beds of Betsy's cutting garden, filled with roses and hydrangeas, which supply fresh flowers for the house. Sitting below the rose garden is the summer house—its rough stone walls and rustic design a perfect foil for the refined elegance of the residence.

The summer house is a breathtaking
setting for a summer luncheon.

Of all the flowers that flourish in this garden, there is no
doubt that grandchildren are what Betsy and Peter grow best.
For almost 200 years, this residence has witnessed Huntsville
history. And it continues to witness great historic events—
like the time its lawn was converted to a petting zoo for a
granddaughter's special birthday, or when a grandchild taking
his first shaky steps, bare feet cushioned by a grassy carpet,
stumbles forward into the outstretched arms of a grandparent.

the Garden of
Lane and Drew Tutt

*Alice opened the door and found
that it led into a small passage, not
much larger than a rat-hole: She
knelt down and looked along the
passage into the loveliest garden
you ever saw. How she longed
to get out of that dark hall, and
wander about among those beds
of bright flowers and those cool
fountains, but she could not even
get her head through the doorway.*

"Alice in Wonderland"
– Lewis Carroll

The garden is a long, oval-shaped grass lawn bordered on either side by a generous brick walk which leads to a smaller, circular garden.

A Garden Where Memories Grow

Tucked behind the fairy tale façade of the Victorian cottage with the shuttered front porch, grows a garden every bit as lovely as the one that enticed Alice when she first entered Wonderland. Fortunately, the garden of Drew and Lane Tutt is open to children of all sizes. The garden is loosely modeled on the famous Charleston garden of Mrs. Emily Whaley; but, as in a grandmother's recipe modified over time, the ingredients of Lane's garden have been tweaked to suit her own taste. Lane's personality — her ingenuity combined with a sense of fun and whimsy — permeates this space and is the source of its charm.

Like Mrs. Whaley's garden, Lane's garden is a long, grass lawn bordered on either side by a generous brick walk and oversized flowerbeds. The oval-shaped lawn leads to a smaller, circular garden, its entry defined by boxwoods. Viewed from the house, the focal point of the garden is a decoratively shaped hedge

The vine-covered arbor frames a view of Lane's cutting and herb gardens.

77

With Japanese paper lanterns providing an illuminating glow, twilight becomes an enchanting occasion in the Tutt garden.

The childhood swing of Patton and Andrea Ashe
invites children of all ages to play.

formed by dwarf English boxwoods centered around a pottery
urn. The urn is planted with flowing white impatiens. In a
little alcove tucked off to the left, lies a smaller, more private
garden. With a diamond-shaped herb garden at its center, the
bright blooms of Lane's cutting garden circle the space. This
cherished garden is also home to the childhood playhouse
of her daughter, Andrea Ashe. An arbor with overhanging
vines separates the playhouse room from the main garden.
A visitor is required to stoop — become almost childlike in
stature — to enter this little alcove.

The oversized beds that run the length of the oval-shaped
lawn are fertile ground for Lane's imagination. Nestled
against the fence, a bench invites visitors to sit. Lane created
a pathway of old brick and rock that leads to this quiet,
reflective area. A sweet face of a cherub hangs over the

bench, serving as the garden's guardian angel. Many of the
boxwoods planted here originally grew in the "yard" of the
playhouse — gifts to Andrea Ashe from her godfather —
before Lane transplanted them to this spot.

Before this garden assumed its present shape, it was the
backyard playground of Andrea Ashe and Patton, the children
of Drew and Lane, and home to swing sets, bicycles, and
Barbie dolls. Lane scattered references to its former life
throughout the space: There is a miniature table and chairs
set for an impromptu tea party, the old rope swing in the
front of the house that begs a child to put it to use, a playhouse ready to host the imaginative games of its young
guests. In this garden, memories thrive and are as carefully
tended as the hydrangeas. And they all live together —
happily ever after.

the Garden of
Kyleen and Toney Daly

Paradise Found

It is a garden we have all visited in our minds. A place where, when the world presses too closely around us and the voices we hear are no longer our own, we escape to converse with our essential self. This secluded garden, a quiet interlude, is an oasis of stillness that invites meditation, contemplation. The sound of gurgling water crowds out all but the most essential thoughts. We forget; then we remember. When we leave, we do not go refreshed, but restored.

This garden, the garden of our thoughts, exists. It can be found on a small plot of ground behind a cottage in a bustling district neighborhood. The garden is not secluded; it backs up to one of the city's busiest streets. It accomplishes the impossible; we believe we are in a private retreat, but we are steps away from urban life.

There is a zen-like simplicity to this space. It is a sunken garden; we enter down a flight of stairs. The garden invites a quiet walk, but it is meant to be viewed from a seating area up above. There are few blooms cluttering this space. The garden makes its statement with green ferns, ivy, hostas, evergreen shrubs, and a perfectly positioned Japanese maple. The moss-covered brick, the stone work, the reflection from the pond, all convey a sense of timelessness. The gazebo presides over the garden with the solemn air of a Buddhist monk, and the vibrant red koi fish swimming in the pond are the garden's single bouquet.

Some gardens invite conversation. Other gardens serve a deeper purpose. The image reflected in the stone pond reminds us that some things are enduring, others fleeting and transitory. Discover the eternal, find strength in its permanence, and rid yourself of momentary apparitions.

This calm oasis offers a quiet retreat for all visitors.

A Star is Born

Some gardens are shrinking violets.
Growing demurely behind a house,
they are careful not to detract from
the historic residence that is clearly
the star of the show. They complement, not overshadow, and accept
their subordinate position with little
dissent. Not this garden. This garden
is not a wallflower, shoved back
behind the house, but has an equal
footing with the home, occupying a
full lot adjacent to the property. It
does not play a supporting role but
is a main character in its own right.
The garden of Candy and Charles
Stephenson is always ready for
its close-up.

The dramatic green-and-white foyer
of the Stephenson garden.

The green-and-white color scheme continues into the heart of this garden. Boxwoods, hydrangeas, and crepe myrtles frame a view of the pergola.

The garden's entrance offers a sneak preview of the splendor that rests below. The dramatic, double doors open into a pergola, an entryway that gathers visitors into the foyer of the garden. Bordered by green-and-white caladiums with swooning hydrangeas, this space establishes the green-and-white color scheme of the garden and provides a sweeping view through the pergola to the urn spilling over with ivy and caladiums. Here, visitors receive their first glimpse of the garden that awaits them. The garden below is very formal, with expansive brick terraces and stone work, but billowing plants spill over and soften hard edges.

A statue of a young woman set in a mound of hydrangeas
acquires a moody, almost melancholy air with the shift of a cloud.

With a garden this large, so potentially overwhelming, Candy chose to use a simple color palette of white and green to unify the space and calm the eye. In late spring, white crepe myrtle blossoms and white hydrangea blooms contrast with the green lawn and evergreen shrubs. This creates a garden that has a very crisp, cool appearance. But this garden is not a one-act show. As spring turns to summer, the stark white blooms of the crepe myrtles form seed pods and the hydrangeas fade and turn a soft green, giving the garden subtle color variations like those seen in a fine watercolor. The long rows of crepe myrtles provide spring and summer color, but the sun moving overhead casts shadows through the tree branches to create pools of light and dark around the garden. The garden suddenly shows its flair for the dramatic—pathways become mysterious passages to hidden rooms, and a statue of a young woman set in a mound of hydrangeas acquires a moody, almost melancholy air with the shift of a cloud.

As twilight approaches, the Stephensons' porch becomes
a gathering place for family and friends.

Both Candy and Charles agree that they love to view their garden from porches along the back of the house. Overlooking the garden, these porches become living rooms with their walls removed. This is where they like to end their day, enjoying a glass of wine, viewing the garden below. But Candy points out that this garden was not created only to be viewed, but to be enjoyed. And she and Charles certainly enjoy sharing this space with friends. This garden is a frequent setting for weddings, and brides regularly ask to use the garden for their wedding photographs.

Candy notes that the space has so many grand views, as well as little niches, that it's almost as if the garden has two personalities: one, very open and engaging, and another, more thoughtful and subdued. This garden is a complex character—capable of expressing a range of emotions that can change with the movement of a breeze.

The Well-Dressed Garden

This is a garden that could get serious
very quickly. Lynne and Steuart Evans
wanted a garden that repeated the simple,
refined manner of their home's Greek
Revival architecture in a graceful way,
without becoming severe. Referencing the
home's period, they created a formal,
boxwood garden common to homes of
this era but introduced flowing lines
and subtle injections of color to keep the
garden warm and welcoming. In Lynne's
hands, this garden is like a perfectly
tailored little black dress. It is tasteful,
always looks good, and fits in anywhere
because the person wearing it knows
how to add the proper accessories.

The sun-dappled entrance of the Evans'
garden welcomes visitors.

The porch is a gathering spot that provides a soft injection of color into the predominantly evergreen garden.

The subtle use of boxwoods, yews, and cherry laurels creates a strong background for Lynne's carefully chosen accents. The moss-covered brick walk leads visitors from the garden's entrance to a stone terrace. Inset in the stone is a decorative circle of brick—a necklace, of sorts—that surrounds an urn overflowing with flowers. Overlooking the terrace is an inviting back porch, with a soft mix of colors that provide a nice contrast with the lush greens in the garden. Beyond the porch is an oval patch of grass, bordered with stone. At the garden's far end is an engaging gazebo, whose design was inspired by the famous structures of England's Hidcote Manor. This structure, with its curved roof and copper finial, provides the garden's distinctive architectural feature—its Hermes scarf.

The circle of brick inset within the stone terrace is a subtle detail that draws attention to the urn overflowing with flowers.

Lynne's potting shed ready for play.

One reason this garden appeals to Lynne is that it looks good all year long and is relatively low maintenance. This allows her to indulge her penchant for potting urns of flowers and composing artful vignettes to place around the garden. Lynne enjoys arranging cut flowers, and the potting shed tucked away in the back is the perfect place for her to play.

Some people have a knack for the "effortless chic." Although it is rarely effortless, it can only be carried off by someone with a stylish eye and the confidence to know when to stop. This "little black dress" of a garden is perfect for any occasion.

Inspired by outbuildings at Hidcote Manor, this structure provides architectural interest to the garden.

the Garden of
Susan and Charles Morley

An Evolving Landscape

It began with stalks of corn, a single row planted on either side of the front walk leading to the porch of the tidy cottage located on one of Huntsville's most prestigious residential streets. Initially, the fertile soil and plentiful sunshine produced bumper corn harvests — and a fair amount of curiosity — but within a few years, the soil began to fade and production declined. Charles Morley decided a change was in order. He debated replacing the corn with either soybeans or cotton, but Susan, his wife, suggested they forego staple crop cultivation and plant a garden more suitable for the front of their historic house. The result is a front garden that still stops traffic, but now it is the stunning display of coneflowers, verbena, daylilies, and the pools of dianthus spilling over the sidewalk in perfect half moons that draws people's attention.

In all likelihood, it was his marriage to Susan that prompted Charles to take a more conventional approach to his front garden. Aside from the corn, Charles had very little time for gardening, and Susan recalls that the only things she remembered in the backyard were "dirt and a fence." They asked a friend whose garden they admired for ideas about a garden for their home that would complement the house's architecture and reflect their own personal tastes. Further, they requested that the garden require little maintenance — and that it withstand the activities of their rambunctious standard poodles, Kate and Audrey. It was a happy collaboration.

The result was two gardens that appear to be very different but share important characteristics. The cottage garden in the front appears to have a very delicate nature, but the perennials chosen for the sidewalk borders are able to withstand hot, dry summers. This same consideration led to the design for the garden in the backyard. Referencing Charles Morley's Texas roots, a garden emerged reminiscent of west Texas hill country. Beds were built up into berms, suggestive of the region's hills. Because winds blow through Corpus Christi nonstop, trees were planted at an angle so it would appear the wind is whipping through their branches, pulling them over. A very subtle color palette is used — primarily soft greens, whites, and silver grays, with accents of deep burgundy. The plants are meticulously placed so that light and color bounce around the undulating berms in perfect harmony.

Coneflowers, verbena, daylilies, and pools of dianthus spill
over the sidewalk in perfect half moons.

Along a sidewalk once planted with stalks of corn, perennials chosen
for their ability to withstand hot, dry summers now grow.

Crepe myrtles, azaleas, ornamental grasses, hydrangeas, Japanese maples, tree-form youpons, and silver ground covers give this garden its unruffled appearance.

Like the plants chosen for the front garden, this Texas-inspired garden uses plants and trees able to withstand Alabama's hot, dry summers. Crepe myrtles, azaleas, ornamental grasses, hydrangeas, Japanese maples, tree-form youpons, and silver ground covers still look cool even when baking in the sun. The garden is low maintenance—both Charles and Susan refuse to spend hours bent over in the sun pulling weeds and fussing over flowers. And the long expanse of grass that loops behind the wooden bench provides a great running path for the dogs.

The Morleys have made changes to the garden, of course. Susan has planted an herb garden—conceding that there are some plants worth fussing over—and a new playmate accompanies Kate and Audrey for their morning exercise romp. Their grandson, a scampering toddler in footie pajamas, enjoys playing in this space, delighting his grandparents with each new discovery. This is a place where many memories will be created. They will laugh, smile, explore—and play endless games of hide-and-seek in the weaving pathways of their garden.

the Garden of
Anne Pollard

Reading a Garden

Sometimes, it seems, you can tell a book by its cover — or, at the very least, a gardener by the garden. Anyone looking over this garden, for example, can tell by the generously bordered beds, the simple color palette, and the perfectly proportioned outbuildings that this gardener has refined but simple tastes. A vegetable garden growing in a back sunny spot suggests the gardener has an interest in cooking, and the neat, well-appointed potting shed off to the side indicates the person enjoys the work of gardening. An open door to an outbuilding reveals a playhouse, probably the work of a doting grandparent. And the rope swing, hanging from the old pecan tree, shows that while the person may be very elegant, she has not lost her sense of fun. This is the garden of Anne Pollard, who is all of the above and more.

The garden's formality is softened by the old rope swing and generous flower beds.

Anne's vegetable plot, like everything else in the garden, artfully blends the practical with the decorative.

In the time that Anne Pollard has lived in this raised Victorian cottage, she has renovated the house and created the garden that grows in the back as a playground for herself and her two grandchildren. While the garden reveals much about the garden owner, there is a part of the plot that is missing. Most visitors would never guess that this garden is only three years old—and was a vacant lot until the house and a smokehouse were moved to the property in 1981. When Anne renovated the house, she moved the smokehouse to the back of the property—it is now the playhouse—and had two more little structures built to provide outdoor storage. With these three buildings, she solved

a problem faced by so many downtown residents in a stylish way that also respects the historical period of the house.

The placement of the three outbuildings determined the layout of the garden. Anne wanted to keep the space clean and simple, so the clipped English boxwoods that flow around the buildings and embrace the space provide structure and color throughout the year. In these beds, white tulips and impatiens bloom. Closer to the house are generous brick-bordered beds filled with beautiful white hydrangeas that bloom in the late spring and into summer.

This garden, like a good book, is richly satisfying without becoming ponderous and overly complicated.

Anne's perfect potting shed.

Anne chose a green-and-white color scheme, both to unify the white house with the white outbuildings and to keep the garden looking fresh and crisp even in the hot summer. The garden unites the old buildings with the new and makes everything look as if it has always been there. Although its structure is somewhat formal, the generous beds and the old rope swing give the garden a welcoming presence.

This garden, like a good book, is richly satisfying without becoming ponderous and overly complicated. The prose is crisp, the text is clear, and its characters are warm and engaging. It's a great way to spend an afternoon.

The building, which was once a smokehouse, is now a playhouse for Anne's grandchildren.

the Garden of Alleda Coons

Ode to Joy

To be in the company of Alleda Coons is to be in the presence of joy, celebration, laughter, abundance — not of material possessions but of friends and happiness — and the belief that if something brings you pleasure, you should indulge. Without guilt. Alleda's warm and expansive approach to life is carried over into her garden, which evokes this same sense of fun and merriment. There is no minimalist, less-is-more ethic at work here. This garden was not precisely laid out with graph paper, sharpened pencils, and a compass. It is a joyous jumble, a bit deceptive in its purpose, composed of vignettes Alleda created for no other reason than it gave her pleasure to look at them.

Alleda's fondness for lambs is seen in this peaceful alcove.

Alleda can sit on her porch and see her garden reflected in this mirror.

A whimsical sculpture presides over the garden, exhorting all who enter to remain forever young.

While this garden is filled with flights of fancy, practical considerations shaped its design. The house had been in Harry's family for years, and Alleda recalls that her children loved to visit this place because there were chickens in the yard for them to play with. When Alleda and Harry moved into the Victorian cottage in the 1980s, the only structure of note in the yard, aside from the chicken coops, was a barn at the back of the property. They decided to keep the old barn because it helped block the noise from a busy street, but they converted it to a garage. They laid pea gravel in a large circular lane to provide a driveway from the barn to the street. If a visitor did not know that a car sits in the barn, he would never guess the purpose served by the garden's doughnut-like design. In the middle of the circle is a lovely seating area, followed by the circular pea-gravel driveway, with Alleda's artfully composed garden scenes arranged outside the circle's perimeter.

With practical matters disposed of, Alleda and Harry freely exercised their creativity. After Harry noted that the barn blocked his view of Monte Sano Mountain, Alleda had local artist Lee Harless paint a view of the mountain on the side of the barn for Harry's enjoyment. Alleda's fondness for lambs found expression in a vignette tucked in a little alcove in her garden. Entering the room through a vine-covered trellis, a visitor can sit between two lambs resting on either side of a garden bench or gaze at the lamb depicted in the painting above the bench.

The twig house is another delight in Alleda's garden. It was created from the remains of an old Cherokee log cabin located on their farm. Alleda could not bear to see the old logs crumble and rot away, so she had the cabin taken apart and carefully reconstructed in her garden, nestling it against the protective trunk of an old shade tree. While in England, she decided her garden should contain a mirror. The window mirror she installed reflects the image of the fountain bubbling below it, and Alleda can sit on her porch with her morning coffee and see her entire garden in the mirror's reflection.

The most enduring image in this garden is of the sculptural figures running along the top of the barn. One, a male figure, has a flower and is running toward another figure, whose shape suggests it is a female. This fanciful sculpture surely represents the spirits of Alleda and Harry, playing high above this garden, reminding all who enter here of the joys of remaining a kid at heart.

The twig house, created from the remains of an old Cherokee log cabin, nestles under the trunk of a shade tree. The rock wall integrates the structure into the surrounding landscape.

A Colorful Respite

Of all the challenges we face, perhaps none is more confounding than how to look fresh in the dead heat of summer. Light cotton dresses and linen suits provide wardrobe options, but air conditioning is a necessity no fashion-conscious southerner can be without. Gardens, of course, cannot retreat indoors. Most have their glory days in the more temperate months of May and June and then limp through the remainder of the summer, unable to stand up to the unrelenting heat. Most, but not all. Some gardens show a bit more fortitude. The colorful garden of Lucy and Henry Brown, for example, thrives on the dry, hot days of summer. Its blooms stand up to the worst of summer's abuse — never wilting, never fainting, and never looking the least bit wrinkled.

Coneflowers, daylilies, and bee balm make a charming summer border.

Blooming pots and cheerful checked pillows create a
summer bouquet of color on Lucy's side porch.

Lucy loves bright, colorful flowers. The borders she plants
are as cheerful as a Lily Pulitzer sundress. A massed planting
of coneflowers adds a dazzling burst of color, while a cutting garden near the back of the property maintains a cool,
crisp appearance. Encircled by a white picket fence, the
garden's assortment of orange daylilies, coneflowers, and
red bee balm make a bold statement in the small yard.

Although the garden holds up well to the heat, Lucy admits
that the side porch is the place where their friends and
family best enjoy summer. Lucy adapted the design of a

classic Charleston side house to fit on their narrow lot.
With the home's leisurely front porch swing and lazy rocking
chairs, it is the perfect place to sit and chat with a friend or
just wile away the day.

Resourcefulness is a character trait whose importance is
often overlooked. When faced with a small backyard that
offered little relief from the sun, Lucy planted daylilies.
This brilliant patch of color shows there are many ways
to look good while enduring a long, hot summer.

Bringing Flowers to the Garden

The courtyard of Nancy Davis offers little room for flowers to grow, but that does not mean you won't find blooms here that will take your breath away. Nancy's compositions recall the works of the Old Dutch Masters for their originality and artistry, not surprising for a gifted floral designer. Formerly a carriage house, the residence offers limited space for entertaining, so Nancy's intimate courtyard becomes the perfect place to offer drinks and nibbles before the party moves indoors. Aided by her signature arrangements and penchant for adding "just the right touch," this small courtyard allows Nancy to live large.

A stunning composition in green and white.

An antique black tole tray, an epergne filled with peaches, a simple
concrete table, and Hitchcock chairs create a dramatic vignette.

Nancy's approach to design is grounded in the idea that
you should not be afraid to try things to find out what looks
good. She likes to mix high with low, fill in with furniture
from her house, and throw in an unexpected soupçon to
ward off the predictable. For cocktails before a dinner party,

Nancy downplays the sophisticated elegance of a crystal-
and-silver epergne bursting with ripened peaches set on
an antique tole tray by placing it on a concrete garden table.
The black Hitchcock chairs—temporarily relocated from
the house—fill out the arrangement.

Nestled around the sunflower and tomatoes, hosta leaves provide
the "unexpected" in this casual tablescape.

To set the proper mood for a bridal luncheon, she covers the concrete table with a white scarf and sets a beautiful green-and-white tablescape composed of a white, wrought-iron epergne topped with limes and leeks wrapped with raffia. She completes the arrangement with an assortment of fruits, vegetables, and flowers—bell peppers, pears, artichokes, mushrooms, hydrangeas—that carry out the green-and-white theme. To serve drinks for a morning brunch, she brings out an antique drop-leaf dining table. The hydrangeas, roses, sunflowers, and lilies in the pottery urn are stunning, but her deft touch is really seen in the way she uses hosta leaves to fill out the tableau—snuggling one against a sunflower and cushioning a trio of ripe tomatoes with another.

Nancy laughs at the question of whether she has ever had any formal training. She began working with flowers years ago when she and a friend volunteered to make floral arrangements for the altar of their church in a small town in south Alabama. She cringes a bit at those early efforts when, she says, everything was always stiff and perfect and encourages people to "loosen up a bit and have some fun" when they put together their arrangements.

So, when planning your next party, don't forget the lesson of Nancy's courtyard garden. Loosen up, try the unexpected, bring the indoors out, and break a few rules. And, if the situation requires, don't be afraid to bring your own flowers to the garden.

The garden continues inside with Nancy's foyer arrangement of hydrangeas, green apples, and Jackson vine.

the Garden of
Patsy and Frank Haws

A Southern Harmony

The garden of Patsy and Frank Haws betrays a southern influence, but a south from two different geographic locations. From one perspective, the house and garden reflect design traditions reminiscent of the American south—a romantic blend of graciousness and elegance that puts visitors at ease and invites warm conversations. Another view betrays the owner's love of southern Europe, with expansive stone terraces and clipped, evergreen hedges similar to gardens seen in the south of France or Italy. Patsy harmoniously blends the best of both these cultures and creates a garden that speaks with a southern accent unlike anything you have ever heard.

The garden shows its Mediterranean side: a striking entry, with stone terrace, boxwood and evergreen shrubs, and the ivy-covered wall of the guest house.

Seen through the gracious porch, the smokehouse, flanked by flower beds and herb garden, occupies a dominant position in the garden.

There is a history of southerners adopting Italian design for their own use, and Patsy follows in this rich tradition. Both regions share a hot summer climate that requires gardeners to focus on spring for shows of colorful blooms and rely on permanent features, such as stone paths and terraces, and evergreen foliage for structure. The guest house introduces Mediterranean design to the garden, which continues with the broad, stone walkways and terraces that connect the guest house to the main house and embrace the rectangular pad of grass. While the Mediterranean influence is strong,

it does not dominate the garden. The side porch with its overhead ceiling fan and comfortable wicker furniture is a proper tribute to a traditional southern heritage. And providing further proof of its lineage is an old smokehouse, original to the property, which Patsy relocated to its now prominent spot in the garden. The herb garden imparts a French feel, but it is matched by the beds waiting to be planted with collard, mustard, and turnip greens—a garden plot right at home growing near the shadow cast by the old smokehouse.

Hydrangea blooms add color and create contrast
against the rough texture of the stone wall.

Aside from the vegetables she enjoys growing, Patsy tends to use
plants as sculptural elements. They allow her to introduce color
and soften the hard edges of the stone walls and terraces. The
mass plantings of pink hydrangeas provide not only an infusion
of color, but the round, fluffy blooms contrast beautifully with
the rough stone in the retaining wall. The herb and cutting garden
in the tiered beds provides another example of this artistry. The
strong horizontal lines of the retaining walls and adjacent stone
steps are softened by the graceful, vertical shapes of the flowers
and herbs.

Huntsville…or Provence? The herb garden
in full bloom in late summer.

Tendrils of Boston ivy soften
and add depth to the walls
of the Mediterranean-inspired
guest house.

The fish pond and the full garden in the backyard
blend to a perfect southern harmony.

This garden respects tradition and maintains its connection to the past. Patsy did not strip the space bare of its history. The garden contains the old fish pond, installed by the White family who built the house in 1888. Growing in the garden are old mahonia bushes, winter honeysuckle, spirea and privet that have been there for decades, and an aged ginkgo tree which shelters the side porch. When asked why she didn't remove these plants many see as a nuisance, Patsy responded they had grown and survived for years—and therefore "had earned a place in the garden." The garden also reflects the connection between the Haws and Manuel Jefferson, who

has helped maintain the property for more than twenty years. Patsy points out that Manuel built the stone retaining wall that holds the bedding plants and vegetable garden to resemble other stone walls built on the property over 100 years ago. Manuel takes as much pride in this garden as Patsy does.

The sounds that rustle through this garden originate in lands both near and far. Blended together, they produce music that is not discordant but a soft and pleasant melody. A skillful hand and artful eye can fashion a spectacular garden, but others are the product of a sensitive soul.

the Garden of
Dianne and Calame Sammons

A Distant Playground

Make no mistake. A serious gardener
resides in the pretty house with the
American flag billowing on the front
porch. It is not uncommon to see
Dianne, decked out in her gardening
boots, pruning trees, spreading mulch,
and even mowing her own yard. With a
push mower, no less. Ask her the name
of a flower in bloom, and she will likely
respond with its common name followed
by the more precise Latin — the answer
delivered with a disarming ease totally
devoid of pretension.

Dappled sunlight leads us to the cheerful
entrance of the Sammons' home.

The arbor covered with spring roses shares space with Dianne's herb garden.

Dianne notes with a laugh that her garden grew from of a certain sense of desperation. When she and her husband Calame bought their house more than twenty years ago, they began an extensive interior restoration that lasted about eight years. Thus began a peripatetic existence, living in one or two rooms of the house while work was done in another part, and moving from one section to another as work progressed. Dianne took to the outside to escape the noise and turmoil created by the workers. But there was just one problem awaiting her outside. A big problem. The house sits high on a hill, with a sheer drop of about 30 feet directly behind the house. With a one-year-old child, there was an immediate need to have protective fencing installed. This began Dianne's introduction to gardening.

The fountain, with a Frank Fleming sculpture, points us across the terrace to the entrance of the shade garden.

Tiered steps and gravel paths connect the gardens that surround the house to the sunken garden below.

Because of the topography of their property, the Sammons have a series of gardens occupying multiple levels. In the space immediately adjacent to the back of the house, Dianne's herb garden, a rose garden, terrace, and a side shade garden grow. Just past this area is a transitional space, down a series of tiered steps and gravel paths that lead to a landing, with a garden bench framed by crepe myrtles and boxwoods. The bench offers a place to pause, to turn around and enjoy the view back up the steps, or take a few moments to appreciate the final garden — the sunken garden — created in the sinkhole behind the house. Here is one of the most dramatic spaces in Huntsville. On one side of the garden is the steep bank of Echols Hill, and on the opposing side is the 30-foot rock cliff planted with lace cap hydrangeas. Between the two walls, is a lush lawn of green grass inset with a rectangular stone wall planted with carefully chosen flowers and shrubs. Guided by her practical nature and her love of color, Dianne favors an American garden with its mixed borders of bulbs, evergreens, and shrubs.

The arched trellis frames a rich abundance of hydrangea blooms.

For Dianne, the favorite part of her garden is the sunken garden below. She says that walking on its gravel path, hearing the crunching sounds made by her steps, she begins to feel that she is transporting to another place.

A garden of this magnitude could easily overwhelm a less-accomplished gardener, but Dianne points out that her garden has been a twenty-year project. Aside from the maple tree in front and walnut trees in the back, this garden began from nothing. Respected Huntsville landscape designer Harvilee Harbarger helped Dianne pull together the design of the area immediately surrounding the house. Inspired by this experience, Dianne began to study and learn more about gardening. She graduated from the Master Gardener class and went on to study horticulture and landscape design. She admits that using twenty-one dump truck loads of clay soil to fill out and level the sunken garden was her worst mistake. Noting that clay soil is extremely difficult to amend, she regretfully adds that not all gardening mistakes can be easily corrected.

Under clouds of crepe myrtle blooms, the bench is a perfect spot to enjoy the sunken garden.

Steps lead from the sunken garden to the 30-foot rock cliff planted with pink hydrangeas.

Although their house is believed to be one of the oldest structures in Huntsville, the garden enjoyed a fame among neighborhood kids, who, years ago, gathered in the sunken backyard to play. The yard was affectionately known as "the camp." Dianne notes that the sunken garden was the last space she tackled because she had to wait for the baseball batting nets and soccer goals of her own children to be outgrown. In fact, there is still a fort peeking out from behind the trees on the southern end of the property. There are constant reminders of this home's history. Dianne tells of people who stop by and ask to see the backyard they played in as a child. She has a collection of objects she found while working in the garden, including shards of 19th-century Canton Chinese porcelain. Remnants from the home's earlier history, these relics are mementos of the home's genteel past.

Surrounded on three sides by steep banks, this sunken garden is one of the most dramatic spaces in Huntsville.

Red apples herald a change of seasons.

For Dianne, the favorite part of her garden is the sunken garden below. She says that walking on its gravel path, hearing the crunching sounds made by her steps, she begins to feel that she is transporting to another place. In this very private space that has been the playground of so many children, Dianne is free to let her imagination wander. Here, working frequently by herself, she revisits the gardens she saw in England or recalls the time she spent in Spain as a young child. The garden becomes her playground, and she stays here until it is time for her to return home.

Each year, many Huntsville neighborhoods are aglow with sidewalk luminaries. The Gesslers join in and welcome Christmas with sparkling lights and a dramatic reflection.

the Garden of
Sarah and Carl Gessler

Views of a Garden

Sometimes, a garden must sleep. The first buds of color signal the garden's spring awakening. Soon the full-throated cry of showy blooms announces its summer presence, to then be overtaken by the last brilliant gasp of fall color. After seasons of preening, of placing nature's magical processes on full display for our admiration, the winter garden emerges.

It is a solemn place. A confident place. A place of regeneration, restoration, and rebirth. It is indifferent to our wonder, our approval, our veneration. When its time comes, the winter garden retreats into the protective arms of nature. Here, deep beneath the surface of the earth, nature performs its secret ministry undetected by all but the most discerning eye.

On a still, calm night, the winter garden of Sarah and Carl Gessler offers a silent tribute to the Spirit of Christmas.

Sponsors

The generosity of the individuals and organizations listed below helped make this book possible. Their support embodies the sense of community found throughout our city and celebrated on the pages of this book.

Linda and Ralph Allen
Mr. and Mrs. Dennis Anderson
Anonymous
Gerry and Ron Barnes
Sally and Ron Barnett
Jerry and Elaine Bentley
Cristina and Eric Benzenhafer
Lynne Berry
Blossomwood Garden Club
Mrs. Ann Brady
Nell M. Bragg
Debra and Prudence Brasher
Susan and Robert Bridges
Mr. and Mrs. Henry Brown
Emily and Jack Burwell
Dr. and Mrs. Gordon Cash
Donna and Mike Castellano
Roy F. Claytor, Jr.
Pattie and John Cline
Valerie Connaughton
Marion and John Conover
Kyleen and Toney Daly
Nancy Davis
Karen Ann Dekko
Mr. and Mrs. Philip Dotts
Dr. and Mrs. Meyer E. Dworsky
Kay and Earl Eastin
Lynne and Steuart Evans
Forever Green Mountain
    Garden Club

The Garden Study Club
Mrs. Ann B. Garnett
Garth Mountain Garden Club
Pete George
Rusty George
Dr. and Mrs. Carl J. Gessler, Jr.
Stacy and Marc Goldmon
Rosemary Goodloe
Greenwyche Garden Club
Virginia and Parker Griffith
Mr. and Mrs. Jack H. Grosser
Daniel G. Halcomb
Mrs. Glenn Halcomb
Fran and Raymond Hamilton
Dorcas S. Harris
Dr. and Mrs. Frank Haws
Roberta and Jim Hays
Mr. and Mrs. Bledsoe Hereford
Sarah and Tom Hereford
Barbara and Mike Holbrook
Nancy and Chris Horgen
Nell and David Johnston
Mr. and Mrs. William H. Johnston
Jennifer and Clayton Jones
Lynn Jones
Mr. and Mrs. Gene Paul King
Mr. and Mrs. Olin King
Sue and Larry Landman
Lt. Gen. (Ret.) and Mrs.
    James M. Link

Julie and Robert Lockwood
Mr. and Mrs. Peter Lowe
Kay and Sam Lowry
Evelyn and Jack Lucas
Mrs. Vivian F. Martin
Jerri McLain
Judy and Fred McLaurine
Mary and Charles McPherson
Jack McReynolds
Mr. and Mrs. Robert L. Middleton
Genie Miller
Jane and Gene Monroe
Sandra and John Moon
Susan and Charles Morley
Dr. and Mrs. Bill Munson
Bill Nance
Freya and Loch Neely
Mr. and Mrs. James Benny Nelson
Katherine and John Ofenloch
Old Town Historic District
Gerald W. Patterson
Carolyn and Robert Peake
Judy and Richard Perszyk
Mrs. Anne Pollard
Randy Roper
Carolyn and Jim Rountree
April and Mark Russell
Jan Rutledge
Natalie and Edward Rutledge
William Gordon Rutledge

Mrs. William S. Rutledge
Pat Ryan
Dr. and Mrs. Calame Sammons
Mr. and Mrs. Randy Schrimsher
Jane Jackson Seltzer
Mr. and Mrs. Brimmer Sherman
Nancy G. Shotts
Col. (Ret.) Eugene M. Simonson
Mr. and Mrs. R.L. Spencer
Jeanne and Stan Steadman
Jenny Stephens
Candy and Charles Stephenson
Mrs. Carroll C. Strickland
Sarajane Tarter
Carol and Art Tischer
Janice H. Turner
Lane and Drew Tutt
Twickenham Historic Preservation
    District Association
Ann Upchurch
Abbey Van Valkenburgh
Nancy W. and Richard Van Valkenburgh
Martha and Ray Vandiver
Charlotte and George Wallace
Kathy and Charlie Wear
The Weeden House
Kay and Don Wheeler
Danny L. Wiginton
Deanna and Ron Wood
Nannette Stockton Yarn

Donations were made in recognition of the following individuals or organizations

Athena Book Club
  In honor of Donna Castellano

Delia Wells Black
  In memory of Verbon Black

Anne Coleman
  In honor of Lynn Jones

Mrs. Henry M. Fail, Jr.
  In honor of Henry M. Fail, Jr.

Lois M. Foster
  In memory of Oscar and Mabel Mason

William T. Roberts
  In memory of Bettie Roberts

The family of Gina and Mike Thurman
  In memory of Carolyn Butler

Mary and Newell Witherspoon
  In honor of the American Association
  of University Women

The family of William S. Rutledge
  In memory of William S. Rutledge

  In special recognition of his devotion
  to his family, his love of gardening, and
  his contributions to our community.

We are grateful to these businesses for their support

Altherr Howard Design

Appraisal Services of North Alabama

Engineered Solutions Incorporated

First American Mortgage

Barbara Hubler—Van Valkenburgh and Wilkinson Realtors

The Huntsville Times

Lawren's

Meridian Arts

Charlie Seifried Photography

Shaver's Book Store

Maxine Sikes—Keller Williams Realty

SKT Architects, P.C.

Vaughn Lumber Co., Inc.

Acknowledgements

Part of the joy of working on a project that has been so encompassing and required the cooperation of so many is that it has afforded me the opportunity to meet and work with some very special people. Betty Howard, Charlie Seifried, and Jeannie Robison—it has been a privilege. This project, and the book it has produced, is what can happen when talented people combine their collective abilities and work diligently toward a goal they all desire.

This book began as a fundraiser for historic preservation and the Historic Huntsville Foundation. I could not have asked for a more supportive partner in this endeavor than the Foundation and its 1,600 members. Your faith and generosity have made this book possible. But more important, the challenge this organization and other preservation organizations accepted to preserve our past is why the streets and neighborhoods you visit through this book exist as they do today.

In his *Notes on Virginia,* Thomas Jefferson wrote: "Those who labor in the earth are the chosen people of God, if ever he had a chosen people, whose breasts he has made his peculiar deposit for substantial and genuine virtue." As I've met with, talked to, and generally just gotten to know the people who created and tend the twenty-seven gardens in this book, I can only echo Jefferson's assessment.

Along this journey, various people have taken this project under their wings and served as its guardian angels. I will always be grateful to my dear friend, Ann Brady, for not laughing when I showed her a book of Boston gardens and confided I was thinking about producing a book like it for Huntsville. I have come to realize that if you have Mary Rutledge on your side—then you've got just about all the help you need. Same with Lynn Jones. And Bill Nance—but I'll return to Bill in just a bit. The ability of Jennifer Jones to make things happen always leaves me in awe. Nathan and Katie Castellano, the summer you gave up to help me with this project will be forever dear to me. And Betty. Let this be the first of many future projects.

I could go on and on about the many contributions of Bill Nance to this book, but it would just embarrass him. I can hear him now telling me to "just hush." Bill, I hope you are pleased with what we have created. This book is dedicated to you because you are the one person, the one person, without whom it could not have been done. You were always there, always encouraging, and always knew just what to say or do. You not only made this project possible, you made it fun.

– Donna McPherson Castellano